Steam Trains

Steam Locomotives
of North America

Fredric Winkowski
Charles Fulkerson Jr.

additional photography by
Frank D. Sullivan

This is a Parragon Publishing Book
First published in 2006
Conceived and produced by Glitterati Incorporated/www.glitteratiincorporated.com

Parragon Publishing
Queen Street House
4 Queen Street
Bath BA1 1HE, UK

ISBN 1-40547-595-1

Contents

Preface

We're both old enough to have been small boys when the biggest and loudest thing in our young lives was the steam engine. As with most young boys in the 1940s, we were enthralled by the locomotive—the blasting steam and belching smoke…the panting din…the way it shook the ground when we were brave enough to climb off our fathers' shoulders.

For millions of Americans in the early 20th century, trains ran in the family. Chuck's father worked summers as a surveyor on the Rock Island Railroad before graduating from MIT—in the days when the marvel of mechanical engineering was still the steam locomotive. A great-uncle worked as a Milwaukee Road engineer between Kansas City and Chillicothe, Missouri. Chuck's wife had a great uncle who was an engineer on the Chicago & Northwestern Railway. Eventually Chuck became a writer and journalist, and this is his second book.

For Fred, all things that moved were fascinating. As a youngster he filled his sketchpads with drawings of planes, trains and cars. And now as a photographer, Fred finds great beauty in the faded elegance of old train cars, the patina of stained iron and steel, the great muscle visible in a machine that exposes its complex workings so openly. Pursuing this beauty has led to a dozen books devoted to vintage transportation, with this being his third book on trains.

Both of us, whether wearing the hats of writer or painter, graphic designer or photographer, are still entranced by the spell of railroading. The track-side aroma of tar, oil, coal and iron are enticing perfumes. And few things are more exciting to us than hiking over and under hazardous trestles to catch sight of the spinning wheels and flashing rods of a living, exhaling, speeding locomotive. The fascination with all mechanical, moving things has endured.

This book is the distillation of the experience of several generations of railroading families, two creative lifetimes and one great enthusiasm. For us, it has been an honor to have the opportunity to celebrate the steam locomotive in these pages— and to bond with three generations of railroad lovers. We hope our enthusiasm will be contagious, especially to the next generation of rail fans.

Charles Fulkerson Jr.
Fredric Winkowski

July 2006

Introduction

The Steam Age

Swift as the wind and loud as thunder, the steam train took America by storm, driving the nation into the modern age and turning the United States into an industrial colossus. With the stroke of a piston, time and distance were transformed. Travel was no longer measured in weeks and months, but in minutes and hours.

The clock, and time itself, was set by steam. Speeding steam trains and tight schedules required split-second time keeping—leading directly to synchronized watches and national time zones. Railroad time was on time!

Like the Iron Age and the ancient eras of early man, the Steam Age heralded profound change. The train became as much a part of daily life as the horse before it, and the automobile afterwards. Over 160,000 steam locomotives ruled the rails for well over a century.

New industries sprang up to serve the ever-expanding steam railroads. Millions of Americans found jobs building, running and maintaining the magnificent steam locomotives and their gleaming rails.

The subject of song, story, and legend, the steam locomotive was beloved; its exploits were celebrated. With his hand on the throttle of immense power and responsibility, the locomotive engineer was handsomely paid, highly respected, and idolized by school children everywhere.

But steam's dominance ended almost overnight. In little more than a decade, nearly all the steam locomotives disappeared. Even the newest and most powerful dropped their fires, towed into scrap-yard oblivion. Their undoing was the diesel engine, an ultra efficient machine with the comparative romance and intrigue of a delivery truck.

Today, thanks to luck and foresight, a few hundred steam locomotives are preserved. A handful still operate occasionally, a moving tribute to the glory of steam.

This is the story in remarkable pictures and words of the heroic steam train, its legacy and the proud survivors of one of the greatest inventions of all time.

Engine of Change

Almost from the beginning, the steam locomotive and its iron road spurred development and western expansion. It tapped vast resources, promoted manufacturing, and created new markets.

Pulled by ever larger and more powerful steam engines, countless trains took newly arrived immigrants and settlers to the frontier. Once there, they farmed, milled and mined products that were shipped to burgeoning new cities, not by horse-drawn wagon or stage, but by steam engines. With its tremendous capacity to move people and goods quickly and efficiently, the steam train revolutionized everything, even warfare. First tested as a weapon in the American Civil War, it gave the North a tactical edge, shortening supply lines and rushing troops to battle.

As the railroad expanded, its ever-increasing appetite for men and materials turned fledgling iron, coal, steel and lumber industries into leviathans. From engineer to boilermaker, steamfitter to fireman, new trades arose to cater to the steam train. By 1900, over 2 million Americans were employed by the railroads, and millions more labored in related industries.

Steam railroads were big business and they pioneered management, accounting, and financing practices still in use today. In fact, the ever-pressing demand for construction cash led directly to the first stock markets.

Steam Monuments

The advent of the steam train and the awe-inspiring construction of railroads — over, around, and through all obstacles-stoked American confidence. It convinced many that humans were equal, if not superior, to nature itself.

No place was unreachable by steam train. Boring through mountain ranges, scaling cloud-shrouded passes, and spanning huge rivers, the railroad brought everything, everywhere.

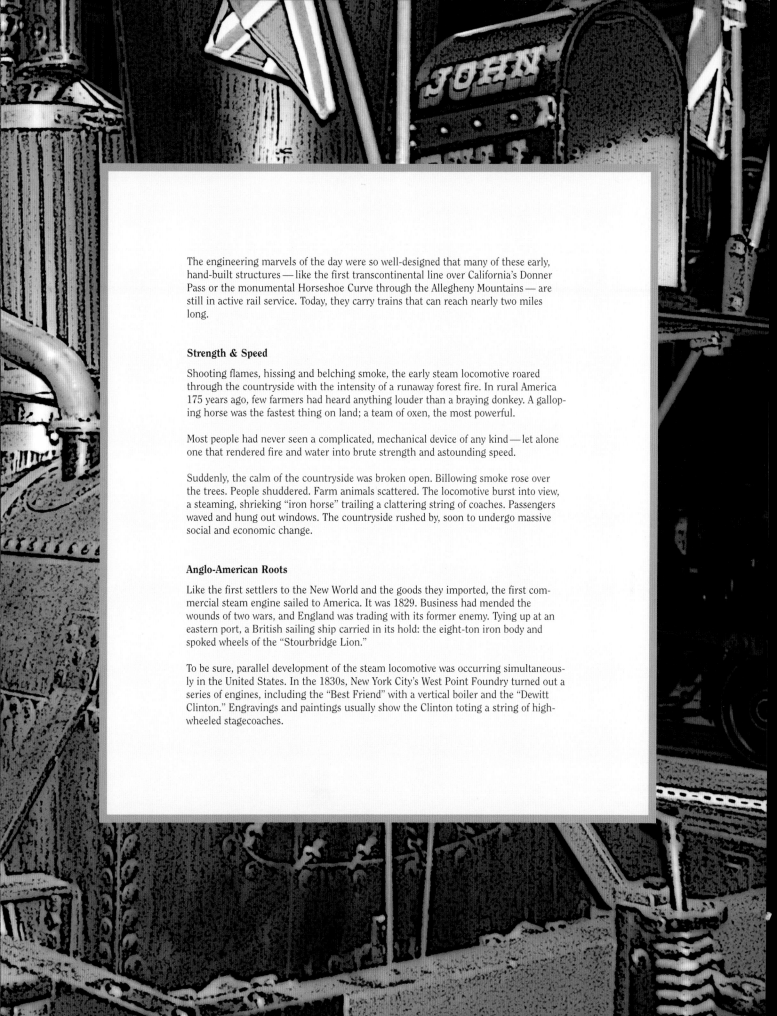

The engineering marvels of the day were so well-designed that many of these early, hand-built structures — like the first transcontinental line over California's Donner Pass or the monumental Horseshoe Curve through the Allegheny Mountains — are still in active rail service. Today, they carry trains that can reach nearly two miles long.

Strength & Speed

Shooting flames, hissing and belching smoke, the early steam locomotive roared through the countryside with the intensity of a runaway forest fire. In rural America 175 years ago, few farmers had heard anything louder than a braying donkey. A galloping horse was the fastest thing on land; a team of oxen, the most powerful.

Most people had never seen a complicated, mechanical device of any kind — let alone one that rendered fire and water into brute strength and astounding speed.

Suddenly, the calm of the countryside was broken open. Billowing smoke rose over the trees. People shuddered. Farm animals scattered. The locomotive burst into view, a steaming, shrieking "iron horse" trailing a clattering string of coaches. Passengers waved and hung out windows. The countryside rushed by, soon to undergo massive social and economic change.

Anglo-American Roots

Like the first settlers to the New World and the goods they imported, the first commercial steam engine sailed to America. It was 1829. Business had mended the wounds of two wars, and England was trading with its former enemy. Tying up at an eastern port, a British sailing ship carried in its hold: the eight-ton iron body and spoked wheels of the "Stourbridge Lion."

To be sure, parallel development of the steam locomotive was occurring simultaneously in the United States. In the 1830s, New York City's West Point Foundry turned out a series of engines, including the "Best Friend" with a vertical boiler and the "Dewitt Clinton." Engravings and paintings usually show the Clinton toting a string of high-wheeled stagecoaches.

But the first engine bought to earn its way— or at least try to —was the "Stourbridge Lion." The Delaware and Canal Co. had imported it to work a small coal-mining railroad.

The Lion was soon humbled by the flimsy track and rough terrain of northeastern Pennsylvania. It was banished to the back shop after just a few runs. Later cannibalized for parts, the Lion's remains were eventually shipped off for display at the Smithsonian Institution.

Undaunted by initial failure, Americans imported yet another British locomotive in 1831, the ten-ton "John Bull." Built by Robert Stephenson of Newcastle, often credited as the inventor of the steam locomotive, the "John Bull" had two pairs of wooden driving wheels. But, just like the Lion, the Bull was no match for the rough and tumble of frontier America.

Train of Inventions

The Camden & Amboy Railroad of New Jersey, the John Bull's owner, quickly recast replacement wheels of iron. More importantly, to keep John Bull from jumping the track and tumbling into the woods, the railroad came up with an ingenuous and far-reaching innovation: a pair of pilot wheels was added in front of the driving wheels.

These flexible wheels guided the engine into sharp curves, keeping its rigid drivers on the rails. Called a pilot truck, the innovation was distinctly American. It was the first in a long train of steam-driven inventions that would stretch from cowcatchers and air brakes to automatic stokers and steam whistles.

By the mid 19th-century, just 20 years after the first commercial steam locomotive, 9,000 miles of track had been laid on the Eastern Seaboard. By the Civil War, every state east of the Mississippi River was linked in a 30,000-mile national network.

More American innovations, like the steel T-rail, reduced derailments, minimized friction, and increased speed made steam trains even more efficient. All the while, American railroad construction continued at a breathtaking pace, surpassing a quarter-million miles of track at the end of World War I. The steam train was so vital to "progress" that cities and towns first begged, then bribed, railroad companies to route new lines their way. If that didn't work, many trackless towns funded and built branches to connect with trunk lines.

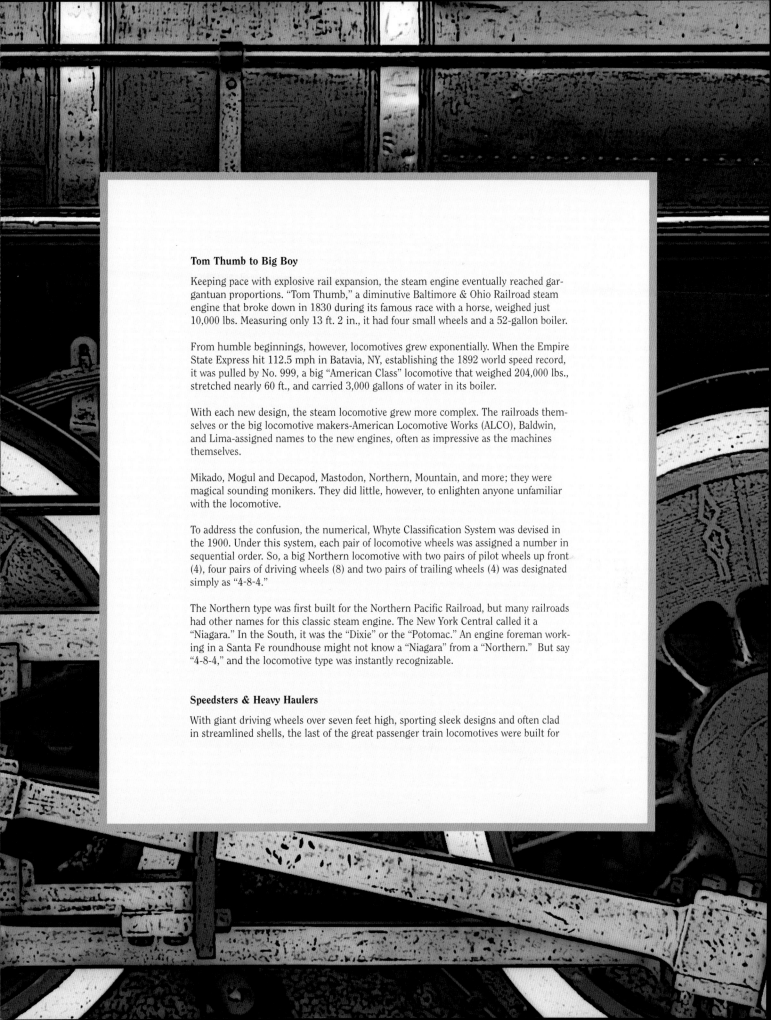

Tom Thumb to Big Boy

Keeping pace with explosive rail expansion, the steam engine eventually reached gargantuan proportions. "Tom Thumb," a diminutive Baltimore & Ohio Railroad steam engine that broke down in 1830 during its famous race with a horse, weighed just 10,000 lbs. Measuring only 13 ft. 2 in., it had four small wheels and a 52-gallon boiler.

From humble beginnings, however, locomotives grew exponentially. When the Empire State Express hit 112.5 mph in Batavia, NY, establishing the 1892 world speed record, it was pulled by No. 999, a big "American Class" locomotive that weighed 204,000 lbs., stretched nearly 60 ft., and carried 3,000 gallons of water in its boiler.

With each new design, the steam locomotive grew more complex. The railroads themselves or the big locomotive makers-American Locomotive Works (ALCO), Baldwin, and Lima-assigned names to the new engines, often as impressive as the machines themselves.

Mikado, Mogul and Decapod, Mastodon, Northern, Mountain, and more; they were magical sounding monikers. They did little, however, to enlighten anyone unfamiliar with the locomotive.

To address the confusion, the numerical, Whyte Classification System was devised in the 1900. Under this system, each pair of locomotive wheels was assigned a number in sequential order. So, a big Northern locomotive with two pairs of pilot wheels up front (4), four pairs of driving wheels (8) and two pairs of trailing wheels (4) was designated simply as "4-8-4."

The Northern type was first built for the Northern Pacific Railroad, but many railroads had other names for this classic steam engine. The New York Central called it a "Niagara." In the South, it was the "Dixie" or the "Potomac." An engine foreman working in a Santa Fe roundhouse might not know a "Niagara" from a "Northern." But say "4-8-4," and the locomotive type was instantly recognizable.

Speedsters & Heavy Haulers

With giant driving wheels over seven feet high, sporting sleek designs and often clad in streamlined shells, the last of the great passenger train locomotives were built for extreme speed. The fastest unofficial record for a steam train, 125 mph, was set on a "Hiawatha" express on the Milwaukee Road between Chicago and St. Paul.

By contrast, freight engines, the real heavy haulers, were built for traction and strength. Although important, speed was usually secondary to power. To gain traction and increase the ratio of wheel surface to rail, freight engines generally had more, but smaller, driving wheels.

Reaching its apex in the mid 20th Century, the massive, articulated freight locomotives were so gigantic that they required hinges in the middle to negotiate curves.

The most famous of these engines, the "Big Boy" 4-8-8-4 of the Union Pacific Railroad, weighed one million pounds and measured 132 feet long. A similar articulated locomotive, the "Allegheny" of the Chesapeake & Ohio Railroad, had an astonishing 7498 horsepower. These engines made short work out of pulling a train of 150 freight cars.

The roaring firebox in many giant locomotives was as big as a kitchen. Some of the engines burned oil piped from the tender into the firebox. In others, a mechanical screw-type stoker fed coal automatically into the firebox. The fire was so immense, no human could shovel fast enough to keep it going.

Although steam locomotives required constant maintenance – on a trip from New York to Chicago, engines and crews might be changed several times – great strides in efficiency were made in the final years. The Santa Fe Railroad entrusted a single 2-10-2 locomotive to pull its legendary Chief trains over the entire 1,700-mile route from Chicago to Los Angles. The engines performed ably, which was mandatory-the Chief and Super Chief were the preferred trains of Hollywood stars and other demanding, well-heeled clientele.

Full Steam Ahead — To Last Gasp!

Despite these advances, the sun was setting on steam. It was to go down fast. Just prior to World War 2, the new diesel engines began making inroads on the steam locomotive. The railroads liked what they saw. Tragedy at Pearl Harbor, however, put a hold on all new locomotive construction.

Once the war ended, the onslaught of diesels quickly routed steam. The changeover was so fast and so complete, that by 1960 the steam locomotive made its last regularly scheduled run on a major U.S. railroad.

Many factors conspired to doom the steam locomotive. Diesels were more efficient, and cheaper. They ran great distances without stopping for water or fuel. Routine maintenance was minimal, and comparatively easy on diesels. Suddenly, the huge, costly infrastructure of coaling stations, water towers, back shops, turntables, and roundhouses became superfluous.

The cost of labor, always the most expensive factor in any operation, was drastically reduced. Entire trades and specialized skills vanished overnight. Even Wall Street ganged up on the dying steam engine. Worn out by the heavy traffic of the war years, the railroads desperately needed new equipment. Banks and investors were eager to underwrite the cost of the modern and easily repossessed new diesels. But for railroads that still wanted steam, outmoded technology was a tough sell.

The diesel locomotive enjoyed yet another great advantage. Every steam locomotive coupled to a train required a separate crew. A pair of double-header steam engines on the front required two separate crews. With the diesel, however, one crew could control multiple engines.

Saving Grace

In retrospect, the diesel engine may have rescued the railroads. Without its efficiency and savings, the railroads might have succumbed to the hammerlock of onerous, outdated regulation and truck and airplane competition on heavily subsidized highways and airports.

With the end of regulation, railroads are enjoying a great resurgence. Even rail fans, who left the railroads when steam engines did, have come back. Their first love may have been steam, but many can find beauty and excitement in the once lowly diesel.

As this book shows, sometimes they can have both, courtesy of the many railroad museums and dedicated steam preservationists across the land.

Chapter One: Live Steam...

Boyhood Dream Goes Up in Steam!

Like a boy closing the attic door on his toy trains when it's suppertime, employees at the East Broad Top Railroad & Coal Co. (EBT) knocked off work for dinner one evening in April 1956. They expected only a furlough, due to slack demand for coal. Everything was left in order. Machine shop and tools, roundhouse and roundtable, switchyard and steam locomotives—all were cleaned, oiled, greased and ready to run. But no one came back. The coal-dependent EBT shut down for good. It was sold for scrap value, remaining in a state of suspended animation until 1960. In a remarkable turn of events, the

scrap dealer turned out to be a rail fan. Legend has it that Nick Kovalchick, son of immigrants, never had model trains because his parents were too poor to afford them. The EBT fulfilled his boyhood dreams. The railroad reopened and has operated for the past half century. It may be the finest example of a complete, working steam railroad in America today. It is a National Historic Landmark. General manager Stanley Hall noted that the wealthy Kovalchick named No. 12, one of EBT's steam engines, "Millie," after his then young daughter. "About that time he'd made his first million," chuckled Hall, recalling the EBT's savior and benefactor. Today, the non-profit railroad rolls on, still owned by the farsighted Kovalchick family and supported by ticket fares and the generosity of thousands of donors and volunteers.

From Black Diamonds to Steam Lovers

Operations on the EBT Railroad have changed some from the railroad's 80-year history as a narrow gauge coal feeder for the Pennsylvania Railroad. Back then, the 33-mile, 3-foot-gauge railroad hauled primarily coal, with some freight, mail, and passengers. Because the railroad is now a tourist line, operations focus on passenger trains. Every summer season, the railroad steams up, transporting thousands of tourists, steam lovers and rail fans. Its 10-mile roundtrip route runs through the scenic Aughwick Valley near Rockhill Furnace in south central Pennsylvania. The railroad even has its own support group, the Friends of East Broad Top Museum at Robertsdale, Pennsylvania

Above:
*On the ready track, a locomotive prepares to depart.
The narrow gauge engine is about two-thirds the size
of comparable standard gauge locomotives, making
the fireman appear much larger than he is. EBT's distance between rails is 36 inches. Standard gauge is
56.5 inches.*

Above:
This pressure gauge was a source of constant concern when boilers supplied steam to the shop's stationary steam engine. In the Steam Age, stationary engines, which were fixed in place, were found in many factories and mills.

Below:
An elaborate system of overhead belts and pulleys transferred power from the stationary engine to the heavy machinery on the shop floor.

"Do It Better and Faster Right Here"

Looking almost like they were left a half-century ago, the machine shops of the East Broad Top Railroad are still intact. Dozens of men once worked the machine shops, repairing and rebuilding the railroad's engines and rolling stock. According to EBT general manager Stanley Hall, they were part of a 500-man workforce employed on the coal-hauling shortline in its prime. They included engine and train crew, yardmen, coal miners, office help and shop workers. The extensive shops were powered by a two-cylinder, coal-fired stationary steam engine. Like many old shops of that era powered by water wheels or steam engines, an elaborate system of overhead belts and pulleys brought power to individual machines.

When one of the railroad's locomotives broke down, fixing it was not a simple matter of ordering new parts and waiting until they arrived. "The steam locomotive is pretty much a custom-built piece of machinery," explained Tom Diehl, a machine shop guide and volunteer from the Friends of East Broad Top. "Most likely Baldwin didn't have the parts you wanted in stock. Plus in those days, there was much more of a self-sufficient attitude that, we can do it better or faster right here." To that end, EBT shops had a full complement of belt-driven machines needed to fabricate or repair nearly every part of a steam engine.

Above:
This lathe-like machine is a Wheel Turner to grind true both steel car wheels and the locomotive wheels and tires. Locomotive drivers were fitted with a thinner and softer metal tire to provide more traction.

23

On the Move

Before baggage cars, passengers hauled their belongings, and in some cases all their worldly goods, up the steep stairs into the coaches. Navigating the aisles was a challenge. Whatever didn't fit on overhead racks was jammed into the center passageway or car vestibules. As often as not, caged chickens and tethered livestock rode right along with the passengers. Realizing they could charge more if passengers and their live freight or heavy trunks were separated, baggage cars were added to trains, relieving the congestion. Initially, train travel was lauded as an extension of democratic ideals. Passengers were free to sit where they wanted. Rich or poor rode together. That was to soon change. Car builders and railroads discovered a gold mine when they segregated passengers into First and Second Class and charged accordingly. On the low end of service, racially segregated "Jim Crow" cars were the norm in much of the country.

Right:
Hand-drawn baggage cart and horse-drawn freight wagon are displayed at the Sacramento freight depot.

Above:
The narrow gauge "Silver State" is a first class passenger car built by the Nevada Central Railroad.

Narrow Gauge Niche

Narrow gauge railroads were common in the American West in the late 19th and early 20th centuries. Many of them were captive to specific industries like mining, logging or ranching. Unlike standard gauge, these lines were not always interconnected. Instead, they hauled their products and passengers to a connection with standard gauge lines where cargo and passengers were reloaded on larger cars. The "Silver State" narrow gauge passenger car at left was constructed in 1881 by the Nevada Central Railroad, which made reload connections with the standard gauge Central Pacific at Austin, Nevada. The car's raised, center roof featured small deck windows that brought in light and ventilation. Another Nevada silver line, the Virginia & Truckee, was standard gauge, interchanging cars with the Central Pacific. The combined passenger and baggage car, or "Combine" at right, was a forerunner of the caboose.

Below:

This combination passenger and bag-gage Combine was built in 1874.

Overleaf:

The interior of No. 14 featured a painted ceiling cloth, shutters and reversible velvet seats.

Above:

The ornamental interior bulkhead of the Virginia & Truckee No. 16 Combine invites passengers into the attractive seating area.

Upsizing the railroads...

Taking a Break!

Drifting downhill with a short passenger train in tow, No. 40's safety valves are popping with steam, indicating high pressure in the boiler. Located at the top of the steam dome, safety valves automatically release excessive pressure that could blow up the boiler if left unchecked. With a hot fire and a full head of steam, the fireman has earned a break. The running board doors are thrown open, cooling off the cab with a fresh breeze. The backhead, or end of the boiler, is the front wall of the cab. Both backhead and sizzling firebox doors are exposed to the cab interior, raising summertime temperature and humidity to almost unbearable levels. In winter, the backhead and firebox keep the front of the cab toasty, but the rear of the cab is open to the elements. No. 40, a 2-8-0 Consolidation, originally saw service in the South before moving to Pennsylvania's New Hope & Ivyland Railroad.

Left:

Steaming hard, the New Hope & Ivyland No. 40 heads into sun. This venerable locomotive demonstrates the speed and power of an early 20th century locomotive, while pulling a line of filled passenger cars.

Rolling Pony Express...

Mail Call

Before planes and trucks, railroads carried all the U.S. mail. Over 30,000 U.S. mail workers sorted mail on the move on 700 routes across the country. Most mainline trains had a Railway Post Office (RPO) car located up front behind the engine or baggage cars. Leaving a large city with canvas mailbags stacked to the ceiling, RPO cars functioned as mobile post offices. Working feverishly against the clock and the upcoming stations, RPO clerks were nimble, fast and accurate. They were permitted only 5 mistakes per every 7,000 pieces of sorted mail. Beyond the mountain of mail to sort at the start of the run, mailbags were picked up and dropped off on the fly. As a train approached a station at speed, a clerk extended a hook from the RPO car. When the train whizzed by, the hook snatched the mailbag. Dumped into large trays, the contents of the mailbag were then sorted and stuffed into slots and mailbags for towns and cities along the line. Loaded bags were pitched out when the train passed the appropriate station.

Above:
Looking down on a Great Northern Railroad RPO, the mailbag stand is to the right of the car. In the car's open door, a white hook will extend to grab a mailbag as the car rushes by.

Right:
RPO clerks filled mail slots for locations along the railroad. Clerks on the Great Northern RPO were fast and accurate.

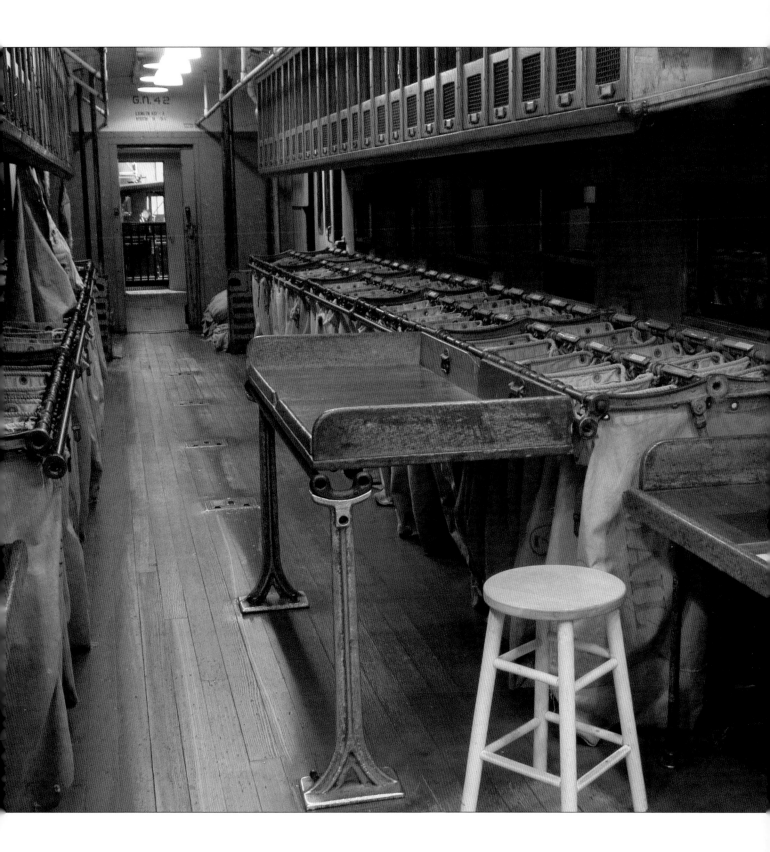

Above:
The sparkling sinks aboard a Pullman are a tribute to the high standards and pride of sleeping car porters.

Opposite:
Lulled by the clickety-clack of the rails and the silky smooth ride on well-maintained tracks, passengers get a sound night's sleep.

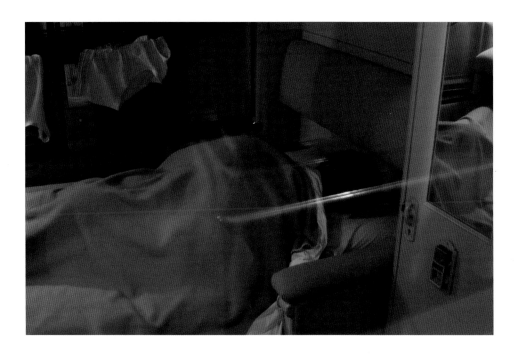

What's in a Name?

Pullman sleepers were as much a part of the aura of train travel as the dining car. The Broadway Limited's deluxe sleepers featured two-level duplex rooms. Some western lines had glass-domed sleepers for passengers to gaze at the stars before retiring. Early sleepers featured a small galley and cook on board. Not satisfied with merely numbering its cars, Pullman named all its sleepers and diners. With thousands of cars, naming was serious business. So serious that Pullman had a Vice President of Nomenclature! Some names were inspired by the Classics — *Archimedes* and *Hyperion*, for instance — and some for places, like *Revelstoke Park* and *Paradise Valley*. Others were named for famous people on the route, such as *James Witcomb Riley* and *Davy Crockett*.

Continuing the tradition, railroads named their best trains. Names conjured up speed and luxury, such as *The 20th Century Limited*. Boarding passengers on the *Century* literally got red carpet treatment. (Every evening before leaving for Chicago, a red carpet was rolled out at Grand Central Station.) Other names were exotic, like the *Orange Blossom Special* or *Wolverine*. Informal monikers applied by passengers poked fun at trains. An Illinois Central Railroad train from "dry" Kentucky into "wet" Illinois was dubbed *The Whiskey Dick*. Meanwhile, the "hound dog" in the Elvis Presley hit song actually refers to a gulf train derisively known as the *Hound Dog*.

Chapter Three:
Evolution of the Railroad...

Bringing America Together!

As a monumental, national undertaking, few projects rival construction of the first transcontinental railroad. Driven more by politics than profit, construction was started by President Abraham Lincoln in 1862. The railroad would tether the burgeoning, gold-rich California to the Union.

Although not finished until four years after the Civil War, its construction helped bind a war-ravaged people. Captained by retired Union Army officers, Confederate and Federal veterans worked side by side, along with Irish immigrants. Once completed in 1869, the line put an end to harrowing, "prairie schooner" wagon trains across the Great Plains and high mountains to California. Equally hazardous ocean passage around the tip of South America was also curtailed.

California had already built a significant railroad network before the Civil War. Without home-built locomotives, however, Californians relied on eastern manufacturers. Like the early English-built locomotives shipped to America, these East Coast locomotives were knocked down in pieces and loaded on ships bound for San Francisco. Among the most famous of these 4-4-0 American class eastern imports, was the Gov. Stanford Built in 1862 by the Norris Works of Philadelphia, it worked on the construction of the transcontinental railroad. The engine was named for Leland Stanford, wealthy merchant, California governor and one of the "Big 4" who financed and built the transcontinental railroad from the West. Looking for cheap and reliable labor, Stanford recruited thousands of "coolies" from China to hand-build the most treacherous part of the line across the High Sierras.

Left:
The elegant but essential cowcatcher on the "Gov. Stanford" locomotive cleared the tracks of errant steers, as well as bears and other wildlife.

Opposite:
Central Pacific No. 1 was named for railroad promoter and California governor, Leland Stanford. On loan from Stanford University, the engine is displayed at the California State Railroad Museum. Stanford's great wealth built Stanford University.

Photographed at the California State Railroad Museum, Sacramento, CA

First Cousin of Thomas!

The Kahuku...1890 0-4-2T

Saddle tank engines were popular on plantations where clearances were tight but grades relatively modest. Like the famous Thomas the Tank Engine, the Kahuku 0-4-2T steam locomotive, carried its water supply in a donut-like saddle over the boiler. Unlike the fictional Thomas of England, the Kahuku spent its working life on the Kahuku Sugar Cane Plantation on the Hawaiian island of Oahu.

To make these work-a-day saddle tank engines as compact as possible, and to add extra weight over the driving wheels, water and fuel were carried aboard the engine itself, with no tender.

The Kahuku is owned by the Roaring Camp Railroads and is still operational. However, its side-rod piston drive is ill suited to steep grades.

Opposite Page:
Framed by the cab front, the brass bell, steam whistle, sand and steam domes are all shown in this shot of the Hawaiian saddle tank engine, "Kahuku."

Above Left:
The diminutive Kahuku No. 3 worked half a century on a narrow gauge sugar plantation railroad.

Above Right:
With no tender, saddle tank engines carried fuel and water aboard the locomotive

Geared Up...

Ohio Roots, Southern Service, Eastern Preservation

The large, three-truck, geared Shay pictured here has a checkered history. Displayed at the Railroad Museum of Pennsylvania in Strasburg, the standard gauge engine was built in 1906 by Lima Locomotive Works of Ohio. From there it traveled to Enterprise Lumber Co. in Sims, Louisiana, where it hauled logs for many years. After its sale to the Ely-Thomas Lumber Company, the locomotive served out the remainder of its working years in Fenwick, West Virginia.

Still operable in 1965, it was rescued by the Strasburg Rail Road. The Strasburg then sent the engine across the street to the Railroad Museum. Today it is part of a world-class collection of steam, electric and diesel engines preserved in amassive, 100,000-square-foot train hall.

Above:
The vertical cylinders of a 3-piston Shay power an exterior drive shaft geared to the steam locomotive's

Left:
This big, wood-burning Shay is preserved by the Railroad Museum of Pennsylvania in Strasburg.

Opposite:
The brute strength and power of the geared Shay locomotive can't be overstated.

Above:
The squat appearance of a Porter Tank Engine belies the power that made these tank engines vital to industrial America.

Indentured Service...

1930 Porter 0-6-0

Rechargeable engines were captives, both to their owners and their inability to generate steam. Squat, rotund and charming in appearance, these little locomotives were indentured to their industrial owners.

Known as rechargeable engines, they were also dubbed "fireless" locomotives or "fireless cookers" because they had no firebox and no fuel. Instead, they had a large "tank" in place of the standard boiler. The tank was pumped up or charged with a shot of steam from the factory boilers at the beginning of the day. The Porters kept running until the diminishing steam pressure in the boiler failed to drive the pistons. At which point they were recharged. Since they were tied to a stationary source of steam, they never strayed far.

Below left:
The builders plate identifies this locomotive as an H.K. Porter product from Pittsburgh built in 1930..

Below right:
The compact versatility of the H.K. Porter tank engines made them indispensable to factories, foundries, steel and brass mills from Waterbury, CT to Birmingham, AL.

Photographed at the Wanamaker, Kempton and Souther Railroad, Kempton, PA

43

Above:
For an industrial switch engine, "D" shows off an art deco livery rivaling streamlined passenger locomotives.

Photographed at the Railroad Museum of Pennsylvania, Strasburg, PA

The World's Largest "Fireless-Cooker"!

So impressive was this Heisler Fireless locomotive that it made its debut on the world stage at the 1939–40 New York World's Fair. It captivated crowds looking for the first or biggest of anything on display. In fact, this "fireless cooker" locomotive without a firebox, qualified in at least two categories. At 100,000 lbs., it was the largest rechargeable locomotive ever, and the first and only engine of its type to have eight driving wheels.

The 0-8-0 was also, no doubt, the first and only industrial switch engine to show up at a World's Fair sporting a teal blue, art deco design. After the World's Fair the engine went to work for a paper company in Erie, PA. Later it served a 30-year stint at a steam power plant lugging and shunting coal cars. The plant designated its engines with letters. The locomotive was cosmetically restored to its World's Fair appearance by the Railroad Museum of Pennsylvania.

Boy, Oh Boy! ...

1940 Union Pacific No. 4012, Alco 4-8-8-4

The steam locomotive grew ever larger even as diesel engines were starting to make inroads. It reached gargantuan proportions with the Union Pacific Railroad's legendary "Big Boys." Only 25 Big Boy engines were built, but they were monsters. Each weighed one million, two hundred thousand pounds. They stretched nearly to the 50-yard line of a football field.

The 4-8-8-4 locomotives were actually two engines in one. Behind the cowcatcher and pilot wheels was a massive pair of cylinders and side rods powering eight driving wheels. Right behind the first set of drivers was another matching pair of big cylinders and eight more driving wheels. A trailing truck supported the cavernous coal-burning firebox and cab. Attached to the Big Boy was a 14-wheeled "centipede" tender that held 56,000 lbs. of coal and 25,000 gallons of water.

Built by Alco, these behemoths were designed to pull 150 car freights through the Wyoming-Utah Wasatch Mountains without helper engines. This was something that the Big Boys did with ease. Although built for power and traction, not speed, these remarkable engines were capable of 80 mph. Still in their youth, the last of the Big Boys were retired in the 1950s. Six are preserved, but none are operable.

Above:
The Big Boy was also a cover boy! One of these mighty engines once made the cover of TIME magazine.

Photographed at Steamtown National Historic Site, Scranton, PA

Chapter Four: Back Shop...

An Army 2 Million Strong!

Work on the railroad was often compared to military life. At the turn of the 19th century, two million Americans toiled in hundreds of different railroad crafts, from hoggers and hostlers to car knockers, boomers and gandy dancers

Because danger was a constant companion and attention imperative, a rulebook governed every job—on and off the train. A rigid hierarchy and harsh discipline enforced train orders and regulations to the letter.

The elite who rode express passenger trains manned the front lines. In addition to the engine crew, their ranks included conductors, dining car stewards, chefs, Pullman porters and bartenders. Premium trains offered barbers, nurses and even private secretaries.

All shared in the glory and hazards of working on *Limiteds*, *Chiefs*, *Super Chiefs* and *Rockets*. Express passenger trains, and fast time freights that made railroads rich, were the pinnacle of prestige.

All Aboard!

Although the engineer was heroic, the conductor was the boss of the train. Often addressed as "Captain," he was responsible for the welfare of passengers and tickets, fares, bookkeeping and timekeeping. A train couldn't move until the conductor signaled the engineer and uttered his two-word command, "ALL ABOARD!" As befitting his high station, an old-time conductor wore a brass-buttoned suit, watch-pocket vest, starched shirt, tie and billed cap. Rulebooks spelled out the dress code.

Below left:

Walking his train before giving the "All Aboard," the conductor or train "Captain," gives orders—even to the engineer.

Opposite page:

Looking like the "Singing Brakeman," legendary 1920s country singer Jimmie Rodgers, an East Broad Top Railroad trainman perches on steps flanking the car vestibule. Railroad songs have always captured the imagination, from "City of New Orleans" to "Wabash Cannonball."

In Harm's Way

Inside the cab of a racing steam locomotive, danger and sometimes death rode with engineer and fireman. Balanced precariously between the engine cab and the coal tender, the fireman stoked a 2,500-degree inferno raging in the giant firebox.

Squinting through clouds of rushing steam, smoke and cinders, and nearly blind-sided by the long boiler, the engineer strained to see rails and signals ahead. It was akin to looking down the side of a huge cannon, eyes wide for washouts, cars, cows and other trains.

The celebrated Casey Jones missed a flag signal in 1900 when he careened into the back of a standing freight train at Vaughn, Mississippi. But unlucky engineers and firemen could also die in derailments, landslides or bridge collapses. Others were scalded or instantly vaporized when locomotive boilers exploded.

Running a steam locomotive was as much an art as a skill. A good "hogger" or engineer ran at speed, expending coal and water like a miser. A 100-car train, upwards of a mile long, was often strung out over hills and valleys. Keeping it from breaking apart took a steady throttle hand and deft touch of the air brakes.

Above:

*A fireman looks backward down the train for a
switchman's signal. When moving, firemen balance
on a steel plate between engine and tender, shovel-
ing coal to the firebox. Exposed to the elements and
the pitching of the locomotive, firemen are
in a precarious position.*

Keeping Track

The choreographed motion of maul-swinging spike drivers and trackmen gave rise to the colorful "gandy dancer" moniker. Romanced in song, *John Henry, the steel drivin' man,* added luster to otherwise brutal, backbreaking work of building railroads by hand.

Maintenance was constant. The steam engine's pounding side rods and massive driving wheels assaulted the rails, cracking steel, prying out spikes and loosening rails. On curves, trains spread rails out of gauge. If not spotted and repaired, derailments followed.

Above:

"Steel-drivin' man" swinging a maul, the trackman drives home steel spikes that hold the rail to wooden ties or "sleepers." This trackman has just replaced a sleeper. He straddles a track jack for lifting rails.

Right:

A small inspection car or track speedster carries a crew of two. Speedsters are the descendents of old hand cars, pumped by two men flanking a fulcrum in the middle of the car

Below:

A trackman's tools are from left: tie tongs, track gauge rod, maul, and rail pullers to winch rails into proper gauge.

Yard Work

In perilous freight yards, the number of missing fingers testified to years of service. In a bruising, ear-jarring process little changed today, cars are banged, humped, switched, shoved and sorted. "Cuts" of cars bound for the same destination are marshaled into trains.

Above:

Before rolling into the round-house, a locomotive pauses on the lip of a turntable. The trainman rakes coal ash and "clinkers" from the firebox grate into the ash pan.

Opposite page:

A trainman hoses down the hot ash pan. Cooling off the ashes before dumping, guards against fires that can incinerate round-houses.

Brakemen hang off ladders on rolling freight cars or, in the old days, ran across car roofs, jumping from car to car. When a car is moving too fast, the brakeman applies hand brakes. Just before the car slams into and couples to other cars, he jumps off. If cars fail to couple, an engine nudges them together. In the Steam Age before radios, fingers, hands and feet were severed when brakeman and engineer got their signals crossed.

Busy yards today have parallel tracks with constant traffic. One misstep and brakemen or switchmen can be cut down by a 250-ton, free-rolling car.

Down by the Station

In small stations on busy lines, station agents juggled multiple jobs—selling tickets, processing freight and dispatching train orders. In big terminals like New York's Grand Central or Chicago's Union Station, the agent managed hundreds of workers.

For a century the telegraph and telephone were the primary means of communication. In most stations, a telegrapher or "brass pounder" served with the agent.

In the meantime, the railroads' autocratic structure spawned the American labor movement in the 19th century. As a result, then and even now, railroaders are among the best-paid workers in America.

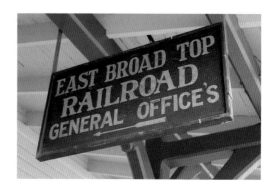

Above:
This sign at the East Broad Top Railroad points to the general offices, home of the "railroad brass."

Right:
An old hand-pulled baggage cart is loaded with bags and freight tossed from the baggage car door.

Above:

The station agent raises the window when selling tickets. Behind the closed window, the agent tends the books between trains. Until Amtrak in 1972, ticket agents made reservations using racks of timetables from dozens of American and Canadian railroads. This preserved waiting room is at the WK&S line in Kempton, PA.

All pictures in this chapter photographed at the Roaring Camp Railroads, Felton, CA

Above:
Morning mists from redwood forests
bathe the engine house at the Roaring
Camp Railroads in Felton, California.

Conquering the Toughest Terrain!

The world's oldest and tallest trees share the mountains with venerable logging locomotives at Roaring Camp and Big Trees Narrow Gauge Railroad. Deep in the coastal redwoods of the Santa Cruz Mountains near San Francisco, this steep and scenic narrow gauge railroad has a roster of seven engines. Most are geared steam locomotives, built for the twisting tracks and tortuous terrain of rugged logging and mining operations.

Geared locomotives are powerful, but plodding. Tortoise-like speeds, often below 10 mph, are the norm. What they lack in speed, however, these locomotives make up for in tenacity—clawing their way up mountainsides, while clinging to hairpin curves. A grade or hill of more than 2% on mainline railroads is considered steep, often calling for pusher engines and double—or triple-headers. By contrast, the steepest grade on the Roaring Camp line up Bear Mountain is over 4 times greater, at 8.5%.

For a truck or car driving up an 8.5% hill (an incline of 8.5 feet in 100 feet of distance), it's a simple matter of downshifting. For conventional steam or diesel engines hauling long, heavy loads, this climb is impossible.

To surmount the steep, twisting grades of 19th century narrow gauge railroads, the geared locomotive was developed in 1872. Most were "Shays" named after inventor, Ephraim Shay. These steam locomotives feature vertical cylinders and a geared outside drive. With cylinders on the right side and an offset boiler on the left, the odd-looking Shay is lopsided, but perfectly suited for the job.

Left:

Climbing aboard a Roaring Camp narrow gauge diesel switcher, an engineer starts his day in the dripping mountain fog.

Right:

The Dixiana Steam Shay, pride of the railroad, emerges from the engine house for another day of work.

Firing Up and Bottling Up

The antique geared engines that survive at Roaring Camp all burn oil. That calls for a unique "firing up" ritual, unlike anything at a coal-fired railroad.

When coal-fired steam engines are "put to bed," hot firebox coals are banked, or shoved together. Like the coal furnaces that heated American homes until the 1950s, the banked coals glow for hours, maintaining sufficient steam in the boiler to keep home radiators warm or fire up locomotives at dawn. But oil is either on or off. There are no coals to bank. So, the crew of a Shay engine "bottles up" the locomotive for the night. The fire is extinguished. After water temperature in the boiler drops below boiling, valves are shut to preserve, or "bottle up," the heat.

At dawn the boiler is still warm, but without steam to vaporize or atomize oil and spray it over the firebox. So, a jet of flaming natural gas replaces the oil spray, gradually raising the temperature in the firebox. Once there is enough heat to generate steam, natural gas is shut off and the steam-driven oil spray is turned on full blast. Soon, the engine is fired up and ready to roll.

Every year, throngs of tourists ride the popular Roaring Camp trains, taking in the towering splendor of the redwoods. The ancient stand of redwoods enveloping the railroad was the first to be protected in America over a century ago.

Left:

Oil cans, to lubricate the many bearings of a Shay, sit next to the pot-like fuel lid on the engine's tender. The pipe behind the lid carries water to the coiled fire hose, which is also mounted on the tender.

Right:

A fireman displays a diagram of the locomotive firebox and boiler tubes that vent the firebox and generate steam in the water-filled boiler.

Rolling Thunder!

Blasting out of the engine house with a full head of steam, the Dixiana prepares to assault the tough grade up Bear Mountain. Sometimes likened to overgrown teakettles, Shays provide big power on a minimum of steam.

In its 3-mile plus roundtrip up Bear Mountain, the Shay will burn 100 gallons of fuel and expend 500 gallons of water. By comparison, the railroad's diesel makes the trip on five gallons of fuel and no water.

What the Dixiana lacks in efficiency, it makes up for in drama. The engine is geared down for maximum traction and minimum speed. The furious pumping and gasping of pistons highlights the mighty struggle to overcome gravity. Accentuated by hissing steam, whistle blasts, burning oil, and smoke, the complex mechanism is totally exposed. In sober contrast, the diesel's inner workings are concealed. Its monotonous drone is efficient, but uninspiring. Steam and smoke are gone, and the diesel horn is flat and dull.

Above:
The Dixiana Shay blows off a swirl of steam, blasting out of the safety valves and billowing from its cylinders.

Left:
Engineer and brakeman inspect the vertical cylinders and geared drive of the Shay locomotive.

Left:
Framed by huge redwoods, the Dixiana Shay pulls its train of yellow cars through a sharp bend on a mountain trestle. The basket atop the smoke stack is a spark arrestor.

Overleaf:
Positioned in the trestle timbers just below the thundering locomotive, the photographer contrasts the bold drama of industrial might with the play of sun on nature's oldest trees.

Boxcars, an American invention!

Freight has always been the mainstay of railroading. The first steam trains served mines and quarries. While passengers took to the rails quickly, they were often conveyed in "mixed trains" of both freight and passenger cars. Old engravings show barrels and freight stacked on flatcars, or atop stage-like passenger cars. Little more than open wagons, early freight cars were imported from England. The harsh North American weather soon led to an American innovation—the covered boxcar. Boxcars protected shipments from the elements and, not incidentally, they allowed railroads to demand more cash for carrying covered freight.

Along with rougher weather, early American track and roadbeds were also rough. To keep cars from derailing, Americans invented doubled-axle trucks on a swiveling bolster attached to the underside of the car. With two trucks to a boxcar and a combined total of eight wheels, these flexible trucks kept cars on the rails. They also permitted much larger, longer and heavier cars than the rigid, 4-wheeled English counterparts.

Below:
West Coast boxcar shows the double-axle swivel trucks that enabled American cars to haul much heavier loads.

In John Steinbeck's East of Eden classic, the Trask family loses everything when their lettuce spoils on a Southern Pacific freight train. By the time refrigerator cars, or iced reefers, like these were in common usage, spoilage was rare. Western lines recognized the fortune to be made shipping fresh California fruit and produce to hungry eastern markets.

Wood-sheathed reefers from the Fruit Growers Express had ice compartments, or bunkers, on each end. Before fresh fruit or vegetables were loaded, the cars were "iced down." Heavy lidded hatches at the top ends of the cars were opened. Using long, steel-tipped rods, trainmen then maneuvered enormous blocks of ice into the reefer's bunkers, keeping the car's contents cool and crisp on the way East.

Above and left:
*Specialty boxcars
included these reefers
from Fruit Growers
Express. Fruit and
produce reefers were
chilled by enormous
blocks of ice.*

Opposite page:
*A wooden boxcar brings up the tail end of a
string of cars. The ubiquitous brownish
paint on boxcars then and now is known as
"boxcar red."*

Below:

"Reporting marks" on a coal hopper from the East Broad Top Railroad show that the empty car weighs 12 tons with a load capacity of 35 tons.

Bottom:

Coal hoppers like these were generally filled to the brim, or more. Shiny wheels show these cars were moved recently.

Bulk Shipping, Backbone of the Railroad

Heavy or bulky commodities are the backbone of most railroad operations. Back in the 1860s when railroads pushed onto the plains where trees were rare, coal replaced wood in steam engine fireboxes. Railroads became the mines' best customers, along with iron and steel mills, factories, power plants and home furnaces.

Back then, and even today, railroads had huge fleets of high-walled open hoppers or gondolas to ship coal and other minerals from mine to market. Both ends of each hopper car were sloped or steeply inclined. This design promoted rapid discharge of coal when the bottom hatches were opened. About 40% of all railroad revenue continues to be from coal. Much of it is still hauled in hoppers with bottom hatches. Unit trains made up of aluminum "Bathtub" gondolas are making inroads on the traditional hoppers. These bathtub gons can be rotated 180 degrees and dumped from the top.

Above:
The sloping sides of coal hoppers are clearly visible here. The cars are linked by interlocking steel couplers. The hose at right is the air brake line.

Above:
Two old, wood-sided gondolas snooze in the early morning. Time has robbed the skeletal left car of its wooden sides. But the air brake hose between the cars appears new.

Back to the Basics

The most utilitarian of all cars, the open gondola carries any heavy load that doesn't need to be shielded from the elements. The basic gondola is little more than a flatcar with low sides. It's been the railroad's heavy-duty best friend since 1870. Pig iron, coal, steel, sand, scrap, bailed aluminum, girders, rocks, railroad ties, concrete barriers, pipes, and telephone poles—you name it, and the gondola has hauled it. The gondola has changed little in a hundred years. Steel has replaced wood siding. Hinged, drop-down ends and deeper "fish belly" sides allow for longer or heavier loads. Some gondolas even have enormous steel lids to protect finished steel and other polished, metal goods. Although widespread throughout the nation, gondolas are easiest to spot around mills and junkyards.

Above and left:
The D&H logo on this gondola shows off a storied heritage. Built in 1907 for the Delaware & Hudson Railroad, it worked the bridge line to Montreal. The D&H is now part of the Canadian Pacific Rail-road route to New York.

Top:
On cold nights, a pot-belly stove warmed the cozy caboose. The stove top kept coffee and fried eggs hot in the morning.

Center:
The back door of the caboose opened to a small porch with steps on both sides.

Bottom:
Even the last car had hand brakes. From the side, the functional beauty of a simple brake wheel is apparent.

Opposite page:
A Reading Railroad caboose is permanently sidetracked.

Handcars, and Speeders...

Above:
*A modern day, man-powered handcar sits
on a spur outside an engine house.*

Maintenance of Way

Railroads own their rights of way. Maintenance is a constant and costly job, generally without benefit of government subsidies or grants. In the 21st century, the army of trackmen and maintenance of way (MOW) workers generally ride trucks to the work site. But in the Steam Age, the MOW crew and trackmen went to work on a variety of small rail conveyances. These early vehicles were man-powered. Most were known as handcars because two men pumped the handles of a seesaw-like gear assembly that drove the wheels. Eventually handcars were motorized, not with small steam engines, but with lawnmower-like gasoline engines. Probably because they were faster than a handcar, these small motorized cars were dubbed "speedsters."

Above:
This brightly painted handcar is the simplest and smallest railroad vehicle. It's dwarfed by the engine axle behind it.

Left:
Speedsters are powerful enough to pull one or two MOW cars. In addition to track work, speedsters were once used as inspection cars.

Chapter Seven:
The Age of Steam...

A Big Event in Small Town America.

Stops on mainlines were infrequent, with most trains roaring by without slowing. On branch lines trains stopped, but there were far fewer of them. When a train approached, sleepy rural stations awoke in a hurry. Blasts from the steam whistle warned of the train's imminent arrival. As it rolled in, the conductor alighted, ready to shepard his passengers down the steep steps. Once all were off, the process was reversed. On long distance trains, boarding passengers was more involved, since the conductors assigned them to different cars based on theirdestinations.

On most trains, upfront baggage cars also carried parcels and priority shipments from the Railway Express Agency (REA). Heavy wood-planked baggage carts were dragged out to the train. Stacked high with baggage and parcels, these iron-wheeled carts were pulled by hand, their cargo muscled into the waiting baggage cars. If the train carried no mail car, mail sacks went with the baggage.

Opposite page:

Swathed in steam, a narrow gauge locomotive is fired up and ready to depart from a station on the East Broad Top Railroad.

Above:

Orbisonia Station snoozes during a lull between trains. In rural stations, the station agent and his family often lived on the upper floor.

Consolidations and Tex-Mex Steamers

Blasting condensed water from its cylinders, the New Hope & Ivyland Railway's 2-8-0 Baldwin locomotive marches out of New Hope, Pennsylvania in a cloud of steam. For nearly a half century, the railway has shuttled freight and tourists on a Bucks County branch of the old Reading Railroad.Texas.

The railroad's No. 40 is a Consolidation type locomotive built in 1925 in Philadelphia and sold to a South Carolina railroad for $25,125.96. It is the only operating steam locomotive on the New Hope & Ivyland Railroad. The for-profit railroad plans to supplement the Consolidation with a larger 4-8-4 refugee from Mexico repatriated to the United States nearly 40 years ago. Currently undergoing a complete overhaul, it is one of 32 light Northern engines fabricated by ALCO's Schenectady, New York shops for the National Railways of Mexico. In its prime, the locomotive hauled both fast freight and passengers between Mexico City and the Rio Grande River border at Laredo, Texas.

Opposite page:
In a scene reminiscent of the 1950s, No. 40 chugs out of New Hope's Victorian station withits distinctive "Witches' Hat" spiral dome.The telegrapher's office occupied the space under the dome.

Right:
An ancient iron-wheeled baggage cart displays autumn biennials outside the New Hope station

Mixed Trains

On lightly used branch lines, or on main lines where passenger service wasn't a priority, steam railroads often ran mixed trains. Named for their mix of freight and passenger cars, these trains generally hauled a string of freight, mail or baggage cars up front, with one or two passenger cars tacked on the rear. Since speed and schedule were generally sacrificed to the laborious pick-up and setout of freight or mail cars along the way, passengers often traveled at reduced fares. Mixed trains are nearly extinct on United States railroads. A few still survive on remote Canadian branches. Until recently Amtrak ran mixed diesel-powered trains on its Chicago-New York run over famed Horseshoe Curve through the Allegheny Mountains. These Amtrak trains put the passenger cars behind the engines for a smoother ride.A long string of material-handling cars made up the rear.

Left:
The freight house and station of the Wanamaker, Kempton & Southern Railroad is a beautiful example of a steam era country stop.

Above:
A later-day mixed train is ready for boarding at Kempton, Pennsylvania. The freight gondola behind the passenger coach offers open-air seating for tourists.

Signs and Signals

The first steam railroads needed neither signs nor signals. Speeds were relatively slow and the few stops were known to all. The need for signals was moot, since the first railroads had only one locomotive and few cars. As train traffic grew on the expanding system, so did signage and signals. Early signs were just placards announcing stations, yards, water and coal towers. Later, signage became ubiquitous. The most common were, and still are, number posts. These are vertical, black numbers on a waist-high white sign, concrete post or rock slab. They identify a location by measuring its distance from the origin of the line, usually a large city yard.

Early signals were displayed by trackside flagmen. They were also posted at busy road crossings. This practice continues even today on some hokey-pokey, lightly used branch lines without gates or flashing lights. Mechanized signals were first installed at stations. A series of metal balls suspended from a mast were raised or lowered by the station agent. A low ball meant stop; a highball, full steam ahead. Long after bladed signals and 3-color semaphores replaced the balls, the term "highball" was railroad argot for express train or fast freight with priority. A tall drink of mixed spirits and ice was also dubbed a "highball" after those signals. Modern railroads generally use alternating red, yellow and green lighted signals. These signs and signals are found at Kempton, Pennsylvania.

The bladed signal has both colored electric lights and a blade to indicate direction. This horizontal position and red light mean stop.

An old, raised iron sign functions as both caution for oncoming trains of trains and a "No Trespassing" warning.

Trains overhang the width between rails by a couple of feet on each side. However, trackside structures sometimes narrow the right of way as indicated by this sign.

Switch signals indicate open or closed positions with red and green blades shown above or on the red arrow and white circle in the photograph on the facing page.

Wood, Steel, Coal

Three key components of the Steam Age supported and fueled locomotives. The great majority of railroad ties or sleepers are wood, generally soaked in a creosote preservative. The steel rails rest on the ties and, with help from crushed stone for drainage and ballast, they support passing trains. Depending on climate, maintenance, and traffic, wood ties can last upwards of 50 years. Railroads once marked the year of tie installation with large, numbered nails driven into the ties. Although these nails are sought after by souvenir hunters, they can still be found on some old lines. Until the advent of heavy, welded, mainline rail, rails came in 37-foot sections. The weight of the rail was measured in pounds per yard. On steam railroads, 90-pound rail was common. Today, 140 pounds or heavier is the norm on mainlines. Although sometimes fueled by wood and oil, most steam engines were fired by coal. Cinders and clinkers—rock hard, melted impurities in the coal—littered the roadbed. On poorly maintained lines, accumulated cinders and clinkers substituted for rock ballast.

Above:
Used ties are stacked and ready for sale to landscapers. Ties can last 50 years or more.

Left:
40-foot sections of steel rail, known as stick rail, await installation on lightly used lines, sidings, or spurs.

Above:
The iron wheel of an old coal conveyor is framed by "black diamonds."

Powerful Thirst

When steam railroads built west, the line side structures they put up were often the first buildings in the area. Starting with the station, railroad architecture dominated both urban and rural landscape for a century. Since every steam engine had an unquenchable thirst, water towers were omnipresent. Nearly all had a hinged spout pulled down by the locomotive fireman. Fed by gravity, a torrent of water cascaded into the tender tank. Water towers were generally round, held 20,000 gallons or more and were made of wood, steel, concrete and even stone. In big city yards and stations, a huge central water tower serviced steam engines from multiple spouts mounted trackside.

Above:
Late afternoon light illuminates the edge of a railroad barn and wooden water tower.

Drinking on the Run

Toward the end of the steam era, a new technology for taking on water evolved on competing New York-Chicago mainline passenger runs. The two great eastern rivals, the New York Central and Pennsylvania Railroads, sunk track pans, or long water troughs, between the rails. Fast passenger trains traveling up to 80 mph dropped a scoop into the trough and water was forced up into the engine's tender. The procedure resulted in a spectacular spray of water that also power-washed both tender and lead cars. Although effective, track pans were expensive to build and maintain. They were not embraced by other railroads.

Above:
Steam railroads require constant maintenance. A baggage cart, ties and tools fill a back lot at WK & S Railroad in Kempton, Pennsylvania.

Below:
Gates and lights guard a crossing on the popular Strasburg Steam Railroad. Pennsylvania is dotted with steam tourist lines and museums. The old Pennsylvania Railroad was once the biggest and self proclaimed, "Standard Railroad of the World."